Grab the Brass Ring

The Key to a Successful and Fulfilled Life

Charles Ray

Copyright © 2012 Charles Ray

All rights reserved.

ISBN: 1478249521
ISBN-13: 978-1479249527

Charles Ray

This book is protected under copyright laws of the United States of America and other countries. Reproduction or distribution by any means, print or electronic, is prohibited except with the written consent of the copyright owner.

For information about this, or other works by this author, check his blog site at http://charlesaray.blogspot.com.

For information on using this book for seminars or other instructional purposes, contact the author at charlesray.author@yahoo.com.

Illustrations by the author.

DEDICATION

This book is dedicated to all those people who have encouraged me when I was down, and who have tolerated my sometimes wild flights of fantasy and the incredible turmoil I brought into their lives with my constant risks and often wild behavior.

PREFACE

Have you ever wondered how some people always seem to live on the edge, taking chances when others stand by and watch, and always come up winners? Think of people like the late Steve Jobs who took a flyer on a personal computer when the computer industry giant, IBM, was convinced that the idea had no merit; that no one would buy it. Well, Jobs took a flyer and came up smelling like a rose. He continued to take immense risks until Apple practically dominated the home computer industry. Jobs wasn't the first, and he won't be the last; people who ride the outside ring of the carousel and risk falling in order to grab the brass ring; living life to the fullest; falling down and getting back up again for another ride.

The idea of for this book came out of a question that I'm often asked by audiences when I speak to them; "What are the secrets to your success?" Not, 'what *is*, but what *are*,' as if they somehow know that there's no single ingredient required in order for a person to have a successful and fulfilling life.

I often struggle to answer the question. Yes, I think my life thus far has been successful, and it has been personally and professionally fulfilling, but when I was growing up, my grandmother taught me not to dwell on such things. I've never been all that comfortable talking about the things I've done. But, another thing she taught me was to have faith in myself, and be willing to take chances to achieve my dreams. So, when I'm forced to think about it, my response to people who ask the question is often; dare to dream, and have the courage and fortitude to keep plugging away until you achieve those dreams; take advantage of every opportunity that comes your way; and don't be afraid of failure. Grab at the brass ring when it comes around, and keep grabbing until you get what you want.

As I study the people who have throughout history, not only been successful, but who seem to have enjoyed every moment of their lives; taking advantage of mistakes to go on to greater heights, and even at times seeming to take pleasure from the mistakes, I've come to realize that the one common trait they all have is that they are willing to do as Rudyard Kipling suggested in his poem, 'If;' "If you can make a pile of all your winnings, and risk it all in one game of pitch and toss; if you can lose and start again at the beginning, and never breathe a word about your loss;" the essence of success; but, even more importantly, the essence of making the most of every one of the finite minutes you have on this earth.

As I did with the first book on leadership that I wrote, *Things I Learned from my Grandmother about Leadership and Life,* I wanted to share my revelation with a wider audience, but as with that book, the problem was deciding how to go about it. It wasn't enough just to know what had contributed to the modest success I've enjoyed, I also had to communicate it in a meaningful way. What, for instance, was my main thesis? Was there a central theme that ran throughout my professional life? After some thought, I finally came to the conclusion that there was indeed a core value or attitude that without even thinking about it, had shaped and guided most of what I've done in my life – taking chances. Looking back over my career, beginning with leaving my small East Texas home in 1962 and striking out into a completely unfamiliar world, I realized that I've been an incredible risk taker; betting often on long shots when others were shying away. That I've won many of those bets is due in part to luck, in part to two other character traits – I've also always been an analyzer and puzzle solver, and I've always wanted to make things better, for myself and others.

So, that's the structure of this book. Success in life, and the fulfillment that comes with that success, comes to those who dare to take risks, but who do so after calculating the odds carefully, and weighing them in terms of the good that can come out of beating the odds.

Some of us are probably born risk-takers – I realize now that I have always been one who was willing to color outside the lines; to not only think outside the box, but to often ignore the existence of the box - but we can all learn to take calculated risks. The key is not being afraid to fail, for it is through failure that we learn. Anyone who has never failed is either incredibly lucky or has never tried anything new. My money is on the latter. What follows is the map that I've drawn for the past sixty-plus years. On that map you'll find failure and success; times that I've fallen flat on my face. But, I've always gotten up after falling, dusted myself off, and tried again. I don't call a task impossible until I've failed at it many times – and I don't count the failures. As my grandmother always told me, it's not how many times you fall down that count, but how many times you get back up again.

I sincerely hope that readers will find some useful gem here that will help them have a life as fulfilling as mine has been thus far.

Charles Ray

CONTENTS

	Acknowledgments	i
1	From the Beginning	1
2	You Never Know What you can do Until You Try	7
3	Success is Just a String of Failures That You Survive	15
4	Where You Come From Matters Less Than Where You're Going	20
5	What New Thing Did You Learn Today?	25
6	Don't Wait to be Told What to Do	32
7	What do You See When You Look in the Mirror?	34
8	Traits of Successful and Fulfilled People (AKA Risk Takers)	36
9	A Few Parting Words	45
	Reading List	48

Charles Ray

ACKNOWLEDGEMENTS

It's hard to know where to start; thanking all the people who've influenced me in my life. First, or course, is my grandmother who raised me from the time I was twelve or thirteen until I graduated from high school. A woman with little formal education, she had more sense than every professor I've encountered since leaving home; she didn't have a lot of what she called, book learning, but loads of common sense.

My mother, who also had only a high school education, got me started, by teaching me reading and basic arithmetic when I was four. Even though the society of the time didn't enable her to go very far in school, she understood the value of education, and imparted that same belief to me.

The third woman in my life, and a lady who really got me started on a life-long journey of learning, was Paulyne Laverne Evans, English teacher and homeroom teacher for the freshman and sophomore classes. When I was placed in high school with kids two to four years older than me through an experimental education program in the 1950s that put kids in grades based on test scores rather than age, it was a traumatic experience. Always something of a loner, I wasn't able to relate very well with my new classmates at the outset, despite having grown up with all of them in my small town, so I found a desk at the back of the room and stayed to myself for the first couple of weeks of my freshman year. Paulyne, or Miss Evans as we all called her, however, was having none of this, and every morning for that first two or three weeks would force me to stand in the front of the classroom, which consisted of freshmen and sophomore classes, all of whom were at least two years older than I was, until I said something, even if it was nothing more than what I'd had for breakfast. This went on until I blurted out a joke one morning, causing everyone in the room to break out in a roar of laughter. The other kids started approaching me to talk, and to tell me how funny I was. In the course of those conversations, I discovered that they were as lost as I thought I was, and being from poor farm families where reading wasn't encouraged, knew less about the subjects we had to study. It was an epiphany; I had actually made friends, something I'd only done before with the kids who lived next door, and those were only arms' length friendships, except for my friend William King, who was also a freshman that year, even though he was two or three years older than me, and one of the older freshmen. When kids in the sophomore class learned that I'd not only read all of their textbooks, but understood them, I was asked to help with homework. I went from class loner to most popular kid in class overnight. When we had student council elections just before the Christmas break, I was nominated by both classes to be president, and elected by a large margin – word had got around – becoming the youngest class president in the history of our school, and was re-elected without opposition every year until I graduated.

Thanks to Paulyne Evans, I discovered myself, and found that I could stand alongside others without worrying about being accepted; I first had to learn to accept myself.

Now, I have to put the foregoing story in perspective for you. My school, Booker T. Washington elementary and high school, was small, as you'd expect in a town of 700 people. The entire student body was just over a hundred, and my freshman high school class consisted of six people, two boys and four girls. The sophomore class was larger; they had nine students. You'd think that in a place so small, everyone would be close, and in truth, the rest were. But, as I said earlier, William King, who lived next door to me, was the only person up to that time that I'd ever had more than a casual conversation with. He and I would sometimes go hunting together in the large forest behind our places. The other person I called friend, a kid named Curtis Turner, lived in the house on the other side, and we'd occasionally talk, but I was never as close to him as I was to William, who remains my closest friend to this day. The other kids in the class room, even though I recognized them and knew their names, I'd hardly ever said a word to before. I'd never gone to parties with them or hung out with them. They were like total strangers until that day that I broke out of my self-imposed shell of isolation.

There have been many others since, some with whom I've had direct contact; others who have inspired me from a distance by example. The late Mary Ryan, who served for a long time as the U.S. State Department's Assistant Secretary of State for Consular

Affairs, became my unofficial mentor when I was assigned to the newly opened Consulate General in Shenyang, China as head of the consular section. I was on my second tour as a Foreign Service Officer, and placing me in such a position; the sole consular officer for an area larger than east and west Germany combined, at a time when the U.S. was just re-establishing a presence in northeast China, was a great risk, but Mary Ryan had confidence in my abilities, and supported me as I 'learned the ropes.' She was always available whenever I had a problem that I found difficult, and continued to nurture and support me until her death. From her, I learned how to be an effective leader and team builder, and the importance of sharing what I know with others.

Colin Powell, former Chairman of the U.S. Joint Chiefs of Staff and Secretary of State; the first African-American in both positions, is a role model for many. For me, he is the consummate leader and statesman, and is someone I try to emulate in all that I do. Like Mary Ryan, he taught me leadership, team building, accessibility, and humility.

I would be remiss if I didn't acknowledge Michael Keller. Mike served with me during my tour as Ambassador to Cambodia as the embassy economic officer for the embassy. He was also my principal speech writer. During our frequent discussions as he prepared one of the many public speeches I made, he suggested that I should write a book about my approach to life and leadership, a low pressure, high achievement approach that got results without leaving people feeling frazzled or disenchanted. In his time in the diplomatic service, he often said, he'd worked for many supervisors, but I was the first who got people to do things without having to resort to intimidation, threats, or assertion of authority; I made people 'want' to do things for me, without having to order them, and he found that approach refreshing.

It took two years, but I finally managed to do it. I've been told by many people who've read it that it changed their lives. They owe a debt of gratitude, not to me, but to Mike for coming up with the idea.

It would take an entire book to list all the other people who have helped shape and guide my life to the present point, so I will simply say, to all I have not named, whether you know how much you've done or not, what you've meant to me, thank you for the support, guidance, and confidence.

Charles Ray

1. From the Beginning

Every story has a beginning. Mine started in a small town in upper East Texas; Center, which is the county seat or administrative center of Shelby County, a largely farming area where, when I was growing up, everyone was preoccupied with scratching a living out of the sticky red clay that dominates the region, or worked in the lumber industry, converting pine trees into sawdust for papermaking, or soft timber for construction or furniture manufacture.

Because my mother was married at the time to a Merchant Seaman who was serving in World War II, the racial restrictions of that era were relaxed, and I became the first member of my family to be born in a medical facility instead of at home. When I was about five or six months old, her marriage to the seaman ended, my mother moved ten miles north to the little town of Tenaha, a small hamlet of about 700 people, where she married the youngest son of one of the notable black families. He'd just returned from army service in the Pacific, and his family expected him to assume control of their properties. My mother, the daughter of a woman who was half-black, half-Native American, was considered quite a catch at the time, despite the fact that she came with an infant; me.

In a town of 700, mostly farmers or lumberjacks, the two of us were something of a curiosity, and I think my penchant for being a risk-taker must have begun as a result of the often excessive attention that was paid to me by my mother and grandmother, who were considered exotic outsiders, and as a consequence spent much time trying to avoid the rest of the town, and, having little else to do, doted on me. I've been told that it was really because we lived in the state adjacent to White Sands where the atomic tests were conducted and the wind blew the radiation our way and infected me. I don't believe that, but it makes a good story.

Three siblings; two boys and a girl; were produced in relatively short order in my mother's new marriage, in 1947, 1948, and 1951, and the attention paid to me by my mother began to slack off. Around that time, my grandmother moved back to her home in Center, and I only saw her at holidays. My mother had taught me to read and do basic math before I was five, so, with my grandmother gone, I found my companionship in the few books we had at home, and the much larger selection in my step-aunt's living room. I began working my way through encyclopedias, novels; anything with the printed word on it. I read of knights going off on adventurous quests and saving damsels in distress, and retreated into a dream world where people didn't 'play it safe,' but went out and challenged the world they found.

By the time I started school in 1951, my mind was filled with adventures, some from the books I'd read, some of my own imagining. In the small, wood frame school, thrust suddenly among kids I'd never even spoken to before, and not having to be taught to read, I was generally ignored by the teachers until I reached third grade, so I retreated even further from the mundane world around me.

The school library had a few hand-me-down books from the white school in town, among them several of Edgar Rice Burroughs's *Tarzan* stories, and a few by Arthur Conan Doyle. Not knowing at the time how improbable it was for a young European baby to survive being stranded in the jungle, I was entranced by the adventure. Sherlock Holmes got me hooked on mystery; Rudyard Kipling on poetry. If I wasn't taking something apart to see how it worked, I had my head buried in a book.

Any parent knows that children are inquisitive, and are, I believe, natural risk-takers; constantly testing the limits of their environment. Unfortunately, most of us have that inquisitiveness leeched from us by the system as we grow older. I know that I was an inquisitive child, always poking into things to see how they worked, and why. Luckily, through some quirk of my upbringing, that inquisitiveness remains in me; occasionally getting me into trouble, but on balance serving to give me experiences that are unforgettable, and more success than failure; a life that has been fulfilling and I wouldn't give up one day of it.

Here are just a few examples of my adventures growing up to illustrate what I mean. After reading in an encyclopedia about Leonardo DaVinci's drawings of a parachute, I tried to replicate it. Using one of my mother's sheets and some heavy duty cord, I constructed a rudimentary parasail, and tested it off the roof of our house. Thankfully, it was a windy day, and I actually managed to glide for about twenty feet before crashing to the ground. Nothing was broken, but after my mother learned what I'd done, my backside was sore for two days. My curiosity wasn't diminished one bit, but I did learn that certain items in the house were off limits in my experiments. I also learned that the house was off limits to certain items; namely the partial cow skeleton I'd found and was trying to reconstruct in my bedroom. Of course, that didn't get to my mother half as much as the snake I had in a shoebox under my bed.

My childhood went on that way until I graduated from high school a month before my seventeenth birthday; one series of explorations after another, some successful, some colossal failures. My effort to learn about snakes, for example, was one of the failures. My mother wasn't amused when she tipped over the shoebox beneath my bed and the garter snake I was studying crawled out. The fact that it was harmless was lost on her; to her, the only good snake was a dead snake.

I taught myself to swim by sneaking off to a pond in the woods; in retrospect a dumb thing to do, but I survived, and was one of the few kids in my school that could swim. In high school, I taught others, sometimes cutting class at school to do so. I'd forgotten a lot of that until I attended the funeral of one of my younger brothers and an old classmate of mine was telling stories to some of my cousins about the things I'd talk other kids into doing; and, the fact that they always got caught and punished, while I was ignored. Could be that people really believed that story about being radiated by the A-bomb tests; I'll never know.

My last childhood adventure; the act that launched me into adulthood; occurred the day after my high school graduation, when I packed a bag, flagged a bus down on the highway, and using the money I'd saved from four years of working evenings after school, paid for a ticket to Houston, 190 miles south of my home town. Alone, and not knowing what lay ahead, I set out to explore a world that until that time I'd only read about.

What follows is not really a history of my life; I'm not quite ready yet to tackle the task of putting my entire life on paper; but, it does use events from that life; things that I've done or things I've observed others do; that illustrate this one basic fact – those who dare go where others dare not, who are willing to try things they've never tried before, succeed more than they fail, or, have success that far outweighs any failure. They are the people who make things happen. But, most importantly, they live life to the fullest, with no regrets. It is my firm belief that anyone can do this.

2. You Never Know What You Can Do Until You Try

My grandmother always told me that the only real failures in life are people who never try. I've observed that often people, afraid of failing at a task, or fearful of criticism, will avoid things. I call this phenomenon **Pre-emptive Capitulation**. It is particularly common in bureaucracies; afraid of being rebuffed or incurring the wrath of those above them in the chain of command, too many bureaucrats stick to 'the way it's always been done,' even when it doesn't work; knowing that they can always use the rules to protect them. After all, if the organization has gone to the trouble to promulgate a rule, it can hardly blame the employee if that rule is useless, right?

The problem with this way of thinking is that it leads to many missed opportunities. While preserving the status quo, it closes the door to potential achievements that are often just beyond our reach if we would but 'try something new.' Those who give up before they even start are the true failures in this world.

Fortunately for the world, there are people who are willing to throw the rule book out when the situation clearly calls for it. I saw perhaps the best example of this in 1969, during my first tour in Vietnam. I was an operations officer in the Military Assistance Command's Studies and Operations Group, known by the acronym, MAC-SOG, a highly classified at the time organization whose mission was to determine what was going on in areas controlled by the North Vietnamese and Viet Cong, particularly along the Ho Chi Minh Trail, a transportation network from North Vietnam, through Laos, and into South Vietnam, that was used to transport troops and supplies. The office in which I worked was responsible for reconnaissance operations in Cambodia, and we monitored the actions of recon teams, called RTs, made up mainly of two Americans and eight to ten Montagnards, who conducted dangerous patrols deep within enemy territory.

As you might imagine, the enemy knew of the existence of these teams and didn't like their presence. By late 1968, our teams were being attacked at an alarming rate, often within a few kilometers of the isolated helicopter landing zones (LZs) where they were inserted.

During one mission, a team of twelve led by a young Special Forces sergeant whose name I can no longer remember, was attacked by a well-armed force of several hundred North Vietnamese Army (NVA) troops about an hour after it had left the LZ. They were in an area with an exposed hill to their back and only a slight depression in the elephant-grass-covered area for cover. The enemy had them completely cut off, with the nearest assistance was over an hour's flight away. The standard military procedure for situations like this would be to dig in as best you can and try to hold the enemy off with defensive fire until help could arrive. But, with several hundred automatic weapons and rockets against twelve men armed only with AK-47s, there was no way the sergeant and his men could survive.

When their distress signal was received, a strike force was immediately dispatched, but the general feeling was that it would be too late. The mission on everyone's mind, unfortunately, was that as much damage would be inflicted on the attacking force as possible, and their remains would be recovered.

The young sergeant, however, was an out-of-the-box thinker who was determined to survive and bring his unit back home. Instead of following the standard procedure, he lined his men up shoulder, stood up and gave the order to 'Charge!' That small group came dashing out of that depression in the ground, yelling and shooting, charging directly at the enemy. I don't know what was going through the enemy commander's mind, but I do know the outcome of this daring, and some would say, suicidal maneuver. The entire NVA force broke and ran, giving the RT time to make its way deeper into the jungle and eventually to an LZ where the strike force recovered them – alive and uninjured.

That sergeant would have been severely criticized if he'd done something like that in training; but, in this case, he was lauded by his comrades, and that story gets told from time to time when old SF soldiers get together. Doing the wrong thing was the absolute right thing to do in those particular circumstances – it meant the difference between life and death.

I experienced a similar situation years later, although not a life-threatening one, when I was on my first tour as a U.S. Ambassador. I had, after consulting with the military command responsible for the country in which I was serving, determined that we needed to have a more robust relationship with its military. The experts in Washington felt, though, that, because the government was in effect a dictatorship, Washington policymakers and the Congress would never approve. My proposals, while not rejected outright, were constantly put 'on hold,' a bureaucratic stratagem for dealing with new initiatives that make people uncomfortable because they take them into uncharted territory. I endured the situation for several months, but the rising threat of global terrorism in the world after September 2001, including groups operating in Southeast Asia, made me uneasy with the status quo. Because of our inability to work closely with the local army, we were blind and deaf to events taking place right under our noses, and powerless to do anything about it.

Now, U.S. Ambassadors typically work through the geographic bureaus of the Department of State, but under law, they are responsible to the President who appoints them. This gives them the authority to communicate with anyone in the executive branch, but except for political appointee ambassadors with high level connections, this authority is seldom used. While I understood the reluctance to challenge the traditional thinking in much of official Washington on this, I disagreed with it. To me, this was like the young sergeant in Vietnam; I would not be criticized for following the status quo, but, if my embassy should be targeted for a terrorist attack and I missed the signals, or was unable to defend it, because I was not talking to the people who could help, I would feel responsible. Hell, I would BE responsible. My twenty years in the army taught me that the person in charge is responsible for everything his organization does or fails to do, and following the rules, when it led to disaster, is not an acceptable excuse.

I decided, then, to take a risk. It was time to do what was needed, not continue to do what was expected. Using my authority as an ambassador, I communicated directly with the Secretary of Defense, making sure to inform everyone in the Department of State, including the Secretary himself, of what I was doing. I recommended that the Defense Department review its policy on relations with the military, carefully outlining my concerns and the vulnerabilities of the existing situation.

As I had expected, the response from the bureaucrats at State was quick and vociferous. I was accused of 'violating the chain of command,' and 'getting out in front of Washington policy' on the issue. The main complaint, though, was that I risked incurring the wrath of Congress by pushing for better relations with the military of a government that was considered by some to be something of a pariah, and that could threaten the Department's budget.

This went back and forth for some time, until I was back in Washington for consultations, and my action was supported by the political leadership of the State Department. In addition, senior staffers at the Defense Department saw the merits of my proposal and I was asked to lead a group of defense officials to Capitol Hill to brief interested and concerned Members of Congress and their staffs. I won't go into the details, but suffice it to say, the objections that had been imagined and feared never materialized. In the post 9/11 world, even those Members of Congress who had the strongest feelings about the country and its leadership recognized that if we were to provide adequate security for our people serving abroad, we had to take a more flexible and accommodating view of our relationships with governments around the world. Not one disagreed with my position; even some of the most ardent critics, in fact, supported it.

I could have pre-emptively capitulated, and wouldn't have been criticized for it. There might have never been an incident to worry about; but, it was a chance I was not willing to take. Incurring the temporary wrath of the bureaucracy was a small price to pay to avoid having to explain to some relative back home why their loved one was killed or injured in an attack that could have been avoided – I thought so then, and I think so now.

For me, it is a matter of establishing priorities. If your priority is to be liked and to stay out of trouble, I don't expect you'll be willing to take such chances. People who are willing to take risks, though, aren't wired that way. My highest priority is to do my best at any job, and to fulfill my primary mission to the best of my ability. As a diplomat, my highest mission is the protection of the citizens of my country. If I fail at that, it doesn't matter how many promotions or awards I get, I will have failed. As a leader, one of my important missions is caring for those under my command. Everything else comes after these two tasks.

When I was preparing to go to my first post as Ambassador, I met with then Deputy Assistant Secretary of State Rich Armitage. One of the last things he said to me during that meeting was something like this; "You can be thought highly of by the government there, and write amazing dispatches and all that. But, if at the end of your tour, the people of your embassy can't say that their lives are better for your having been there, you're a (expletive deleted) failure." He's absolutely right; you can go through your career, getting promotions and receiving accolades, but if at the end of that career, the people you have touched can't say that you had a positive effect on their lives, if you have done nothing to leave if organization a little better than you found it, your career will have been a failure.

Not everything is possible. As you try new things, you will fail; you will often fall flat on your face. But, it's not important how many times you fall down, only how many times you get back up and keep pushing forward. Success is nothing but a string of mishaps that you survive and learn from. Until you try, you will never know what you can do.

Abraham Lincoln, 'The Great Emancipator,' took great risks in his efforts to keep the Union together.

3. Success is Just a String of Failures That You Survive

How do you define success? Is it getting everything right the first time you try; never suffering the sting of defeat?

If this is how you view success, I fear you are missing a lot of the beauty that life has to offer. There are, I suppose, some lucky few people for whom life never throws curves, who have everything simply fall into their laps, ready-made and pre-packaged. I've never met one of these people, though. Those I've encountered who claim to have never failed have either been self-deluded liars, or people who have never tried to do anything new, and who have never achieved anything truly worthwhile.

True success consists not of lack of ever failing, but of persisting until you prevail; of falling down repeatedly; and just as repeatedly, getting back up and making another effort.

Consider the case of Abraham Lincoln, our sixteenth president, and the man who saved the fledgling union. By all accounts, Lincoln was a successful president, regarded as one of the best, if not the best, this country has ever produced. But, Lincoln's life story is not one of success after success. Before becoming president, Lincoln's life was one failure after another.

Beginning in 1832, Lincoln had as many failures as successes. That year, for instance, although he was elected company captain of the Illinois militia in the Black Hawk War, he was defeated in his run for the Illinois legislature. He failed in business the following year, even though he was appointed postmaster of New Salem, Illinois and deputy surveyor for Sangamon County. He finally won a seat in the state legislature in 1834, but his sweetheart died the following year, and in 1936, he suffered a nervous breakdown. In 1838 he was defeated in his bid to become speaker of the legislature and in 1843 he lost his first run for the U.S. Congress. He was finally elected to Congress in 1846, but lost his seat two years later when he acceded to the Whip Party rule on seat rotation and declined to run for re-election. In 1854 he was defeated when he ran for a seat in the U.S. Senate, and defeated again in 1855 when he sought the vice presidential nomination of his party. His losses didn't end there; he lost in his second bid for a Senate seat in 1858. While Lincoln had a few small successes during this tumultuous 26-year period, his failures were such that it would be hard for anyone unfamiliar with American history to believe that he would be elected president in 1860; but, he did.

What was the secret of Abraham Lincoln's success? That he was intelligent, there is little doubt; and that he was a capable and effective leader was demonstrated during the Civil War that followed closely upon his election. But, I believe the greatest factor in his success was his refusal to give up. Lincoln said, "I walk slowly, but I never walk backward." He fell down a lot, but he always got back up. Lincoln didn't see failure as the end, but as a starting point for renewed effort. In the words of Havelock Ellis, "It is on our failures that we base a new and different and better success."

Failure is not the worst thing that can happen to us; the worst thing is never to have tried at all. There can be no better example of this than the man who ranks as the greatest public figure in American history, a great leader, an eloquent orator, and an effective politician, the sixteenth President of the United States, A. Lincoln.

But, it was not just persistence alone that made Lincoln great. A close reading of the history of this great man will also show that he was willing to take great risks when the stakes were high. He often made mistakes in the selection of the general to prosecute the war, but he was willing to learn from those mistakes. He took a great political risk, for instance, when he fired Major General George B. McClellan because of his timidity and failure to lead the Army of the Potomac to victories. When Lincoln issued the Emancipation Proclamation, he was careful to avoid offending those slaveholding states that had remained in the Union by only freeing slaves in those states that were part of the insurrection. In doing this, he knew that he risked losing the support of abolitionists, and his order countermanding efforts by some of his army commanders to ban slavery in their areas of operation risked alienating them as well. But, Lincoln's main goal was to successfully prosecute the war and save the Union while, at the same time, maintaining the loyalty of his primary constituency, the ordinary citizens of the northern and western states. Some historians still judge him harshly for this move, but the final outcome proved his course action to be the right one.

You can chose the path others have taken, or you can blaze your own trail for others to follow. The choice is yours.

4. Where You Come From Matters Less Than Where You're Going

During my last assignment as a U.S. Ambassador, one of my main goals was to establish effective communications with the youth of that country who make up the majority of the population, and who are the best hope for the eventual restoration of rational, representative government. One of the things that struck me after I'd been in the country for a few months was what appeared to be an obsession with the past; no conversation lasted for more than a few minutes before the sins, real and imagined, or sometimes fabricated, were brought up. This struck me as unhealthy for young people who should be firmly focused on the future.

One of the responses I crafted to address this issue was a series of opinion pieces, which were first posted on the Embassy's Web Site and Facebook page. Soon, the local independent media started requesting permission to publish them. Within a few months, I had become a fairly regular feature on the editorial pages of the independent press. While I aimed my articles primarily at young people, the messages they contained applied to everyone. My message, emphasized in each article, was simple: while your origins are important because they help to shape into the person you are, the really important thing in life is the destination, which your actions and choices determine. Becoming mired in the past, obsessing about things that you cannot change, not only distorts the present, but mortgages the future.

My message caught on, and my editorials generated a lot of buzz around the country. My staff decided to take twenty or of their favorites and publish them in a little book for distribution to schools and youth groups. In honor of my grandmother, and paraphrasing something I remember her saying when I was young, he book was entitled, *Where you come from matters less than where you're going.* Published in 2010, first in English, demand was so great the first press run of a couple thousand copies was gone in a few months. A second press run was gobbled up almost as quickly, and request for copies continued to pour in. We decided to issue the book in the local languages as well, and in early 2012, vernacular editions were available.

Throughout the book, and in all of my public speeches and other writing, I continued to emphasize some basic principles; we are each responsible for our own destiny; while where we come from and the things we experience as we pass through this life are not unimportant, they are far less important than the goals we set and the actions and choices we undertake in pursuit of those goals. I'd like to think this small book has made a difference in at least one young person's life.

Now, you might well ask, what does any of this have to with risk taking?

To most people, the past is known, and even when that past was not all that we would have wished it to be, it seems somehow safe and comfortable. The future, on the other hand, is unseen and unknown, and therefore, uncomfortable. How often have you heard someone speaking nostalgically of the 'good old days?'

I am no behavioral scientist, but from decades of observation and interacting with such people, I have come to the conclusion that this is a result of our mind's tendency to edit memories. For the most part, we seem to choose to remember the good things and edit out, or dampen, the unpleasant memories. If we would only remove the filters, we would see that the 'good old days' were a mixture of both good and bad. I can, for instance, easily recall the best days of my childhood; the summers fishing in the stream that ran behind our house, or romping through the woods with my best friend and high school classmate, William. But, I have long since removed the filters, so I also recall the social restrictions that black people of that era suffered; having to wait in a store for all whites to be served first, not being able to eat in the town's only restaurant, or having to get your food served to you in the kitchen or our of a side window marked 'Colored.' I remember never having anything but hand-me-down books and equipment from the white school until high school when the curriculum was changed and the school district had to buy new books for everyone.

While the 'good old days' had their nice points, they weren't really all that 'good.'

You can't go back and change the past; nor should you. It is where you came from, and in many ways, it has provided the basic shape of who you are. Where you are is the present, and every tomorrow is the future; and whether you like it or not, that is where you're bound. What you can do is use the past, good and bad, to make things better in the present. And, while you're doing that, you should be focusing on where you're going. Walking toward the future with your eyes on the past is a sure way to fall flat.

Open doors and enter strange rooms; walk the path that no one has walked before. Go boldly into the unknown, and get to know it. Is that risky? You bet your life it is. But, in my humble and unscientific opinion, it is less of a risk in the end than backing into the future.

It's said that Opportunity knocks but once. I disagree; Opportunity is already inside with the goodies and has no need to knock. You have to kick the door in and take your opportunities.

1. What New Thing Did You Learn Today?

When I speak with young people about leadership, one of the things I tell them is that learning should be a life-long pursuit. When you stop learning, you stop growing, and continued growth should be one of your life goals.

But, when I talk about learning, to me, it means much more than just the classroom type of education. In order to live a life that is both successful and fulfilling, you must also continue to expand your horizons. You have to 'grab the brass ring' every day of your life if you want to live that life to the fullest.

I always tell my young listeners that they should commit to learning at least one new thing every day; or at least, start learning. And, if you want to get the most from the learning experience, make that new thing something you've never done before.

When I was eight, we lived in my step-father's home town, a few miles from his old home which at the time was occupied by his older sister. A taciturn woman, she barely tolerated other people, and kept all the furniture in her living room covered in plastic, and never allowed anyone to use it. In that living room, she had a bookcase which contained a complete set of the *Encyclopedia Britannica*, which from the pristine condition of the books, had never been read. By that time, I was in third grade, and had read everyone of the small collection of books in the school library, including every issue of *National Geographic* from 1948 to 1952. Both my mother and step-father worked, but their combined incomes was barely enough to keep the family fed and pay the rent on the little hovel we lived in, so buying books was out of the question.

One Sunday, when we were visiting my step-aunt, while the adults were talking about whatever it was they talked about, I sneaked away and invaded her *sanctum sanctorum*. My objective was that set of encyclopedias. Aunt Rosie, with a surprised look on her light brown face, caught me just as I was about 20 pages into the first volume. I expected her to pitch a hissy fit, but instead, she was so impressed that I could actually read the thing – she tested me to make sure – she decided on the spot that the restriction on entering the living room no longer applied to me. Not even her husband, Sullivan, was allowed in the living room, but I was. Her only requirement was that I take my shoes off before entering, and that I sit on the floor to read, not on her never-used chairs. I didn't care; I would have perched on the roof for a chance at all that knowledge.

I give all that background, not because it's about learning something new; not even because it's about taking risks – despite the fact that invading that pristine room wasn't a risk, I could have got the tanning of my life for that little escapade – but, because of what happened next.

I read every one of those books from cover to cover, reading about things I had only imagined, and many things that I'd never known existed. But it was the third volume that caught my eye. It had an article on Chess; the history of the game and instructions on how to play it. Now, it's safe to say that among the 700 or so inhabitants of Tenaha, Texas, there was not one who had ever played chess; or even thought about playing it. The game was too cerebral, too complex. I'd never heard of it before; but, I was determined to learn it.

My first problem, though, was where to get a chess board and men. It was a little tricky, but I drew squares on an old piece of cardboard and fashioned chess pieces with the sticky red clay that is everywhere in Shelby County. They weren't works of art, but fairly close in resemblance to the pictures in the book, and after they'd dried in the hot sun for a few days, I set about playing my first game. Over and over, I copied the famous games that were described in the encyclopedia until I was satisfied that I understood the basics of chess – as well as an eight-year-old can understand anything. Now, I'm not, nor will I ever be, a chess master. A smart twelve-year-old can beat me in twenty moves. But, that exercise gave me much more. As I struggled with openings, middle games, and closing games, I learned how to anticipate the moves of an opponent, how to look far ahead of the current move, how to break complex problems into their simplest components; skills that have served me well in all the years since, professionally and personally, enabling me to take on unfamiliar tasks without worrying overmuch, because I had the skills and confidence to tackle them.

I realized the benefits of picking up stray knowledge during my first assignment as a Foreign Service Officer in 1984. My first posting after training began in 1963, and was to China, where I was assigned, as all first tour officers were, to the Visa Section. I spent eight to ten hours a day, five days a week, interviewing Chinese who sought to emigrate to the United States, replacing passports for American citizens who had misplaced that precious document somewhere during their travels, and trying to determine which of the applicants for visas as specialty chefs were valid and which were trying to run a scam on us. During the early part of my tour, the Department of State decided to come into the 20th century and start using computers in its operations. The system at the time was the Wang, a clunky set of hardware attached by miles of cable to a noisy central processing unit. The problem was, they sent us the equipment, along with all the instruction manuals, but no one in Guangzhou had ever used a computer before, much less installed a complete system. No one, that is, except me.

In high school, I was something of a nerd. I was always ordering strange kits from the Edmund Scientific catalog, and then scaring the bejeezus out of my mother by assembling things that whirred, whistled and smoked. One of the things I ordered was an analog computer kit that operated on batteries. After much trial and error, I actually got it to work after a fashion, but in the process, I learned a lot about how computers work. Because of that experience, when I was in the army, for a brief period after I was commissioned I was an artillery officer, I was selected to work with a new computerized fire control system, called Fire Direction and Control, or FADAC, an analog computer that was designed to replace the manual slide rule-like mechanisms we had been using. FADAC's operation was similar enough to the computer I'd built in high school, I learned to operate it much faster than any of the other officers assigned to the project, and became de facto project leader.

When the Wang computers arrived, the boxes of equipment and books were consigned to the warehouse. No one knew what to do with them, and no one seemed to want to have anything to do with them. I asked my supervisor, Elizabeth 'Liz' Raspolic, if I could take some of the books home at night and see if I could figure the system out. It was different from my little home-built computer, and FADAC as well, but the instructions were relatively straight forward. After a few nights of poring over the manuals, I was confident that I could put the system together, and make it work. I approached Liz and asked her to get the Consul General's permission for me to install the system.

To my surprise, Wever Gim, the Consul General at that time, agreed. It turned out that the hardest part of the operation was running the cables from the central processor, which was on the ground floor of an old Russian-style Hotel, which housed the Consulate

General and our apartments, to his office, which was on the seventh or eighth floor. But, after a few weeks of pulling and securing cables, the system was up and running and I'd gotten a reputation as a computer expert. That designation followed me for my next three duty tours. It wasn't until later that systems management became a specialty career field in the State Department; systems managers were usually chosen from among qualified family members accompanying their Foreign Service spouses; and, as a generalist, I wasn't about to apply to be a specialist, but, I had the honor to be among the vanguard of those who introduced IT to American diplomacy. There were no awards given to those of us who worked with the cumbersome machines in the early days, but that doesn't lessen the pride in what we achieved.

Had I not decided in high school that I wanted to learn about this strange machine called a computer, that never would have happened.

So, my advice is, don't forget the past, but don't try to live in it either. Keep your eyes and efforts firmly focused on the future; grab the brass ring and hang on for the ride.

Grab the Brass Ring

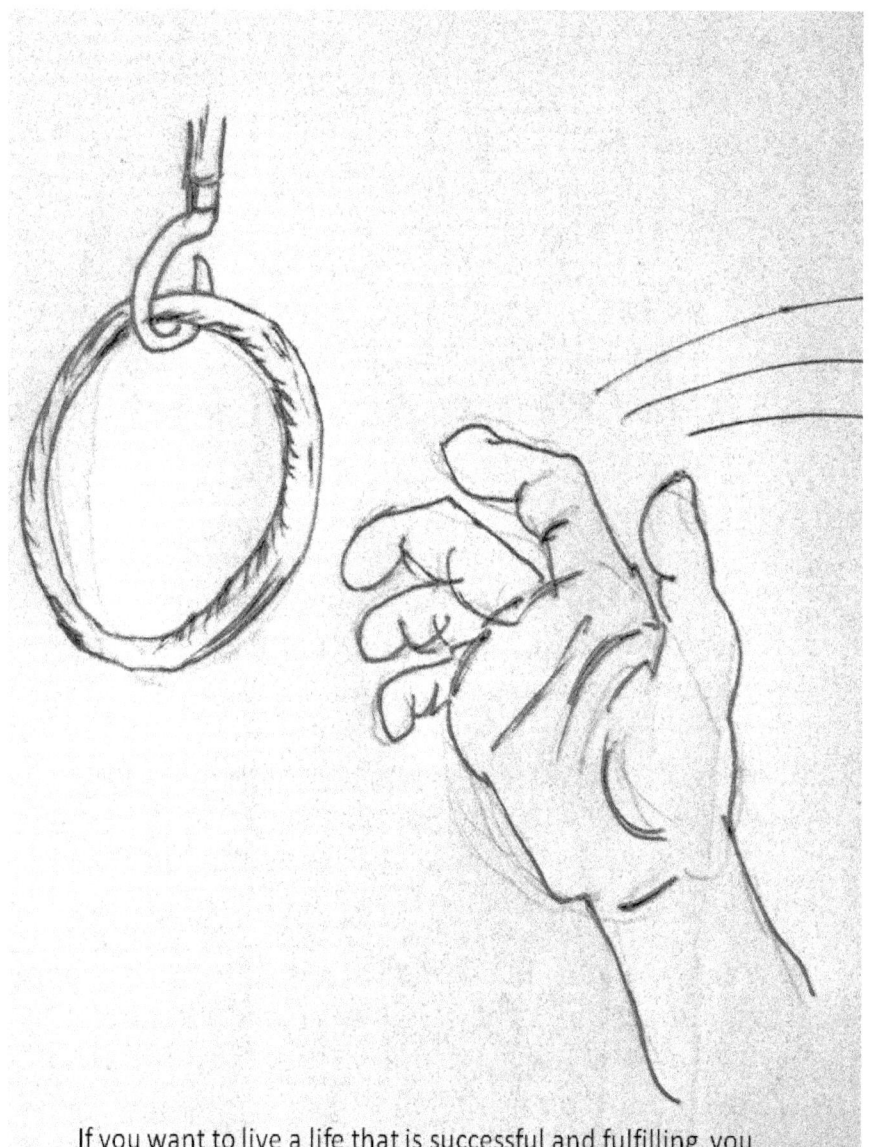

If you want to live a life that is successful and fulfilling, you have to 'go for the brass ring.'

5. Don't Wait To Be Told What To Do

One common trait that I have observed in many timid people who are afraid to try anything new – and, this seems to be unfortunately common in bureaucrats – is that they will seldom initiate anything. They are often very good at following standing orders, or doing things according to well-established procedure; everything is 'by the book.' Even when the situation calls for a different approach, these people will do 'what they've always done, or been told to do.'

When people like this are faced with changed circumstances and they follow procedure and it fails, their answer is always, 'that's procedure; it's not my fault that it doesn't work.'

The fact is, though, while it's not their fault that the traditional way doesn't work, it is their fault for failing to try a different way.

When things go wrong, or just go along in a mediocre manner, never changing, never improving, risk takers are willing to 'try something new.'

When an experiment didn't pan out, as Thomas Edison was seeking to make a light bulb, he didn't throw up his hands and moan; he just tried another way until he achieved his goal. Had he been a traditional bureaucrat, in the mold of those we encounter every day who tell us 'those are the rules,' we would probably been reading books like this by lamp light for much longer than we did.

If people like Bill Gates, or the late Steve Jobs, had waited to build portable computers, only after the computer industry, which was convinced that people didn't want computers in their homes, we might not have the i-Pods, i-Pads, Tablets, and other technological innovations that we now take for granted.

Henry Ford didn't wait for someone to tell him that assembly line production of automobiles made it possible to build cars cheaper, enabling working class American families to buy a 'horseless carriage.' He took the risk, and the world has been forever changed by it.

What you get out of life depends on the choices you make. If you wait to be told what to do, you're not making choices; you're allowing someone else, or the system, to make choices for you. Is that the kind of life you aspire to?

7. What Do You See When You Look in The Mirror?

The act of taking risks, and I must stress here that I don't mean wild flings, but managed risks after weighing the positives and negatives, requires one thing very important; a good understanding of yourself.

What are your greatest strengths? In what areas do you fall short? If you're afraid of heights, as I am, you'll want to prepare well before taking up rock climbing or sky diving. If you can't hold your breath for more than fifteen seconds or so, snorkeling might not be advised until you've improved your lung capacity.

More importantly, even, when you look in the mirror, do you trust the person you see? Is that image staring back at you the kind of person you'd recommend to others as trustworthy and reliable?

If you doubt yourself, risk taking is, well, risky. If you're not sure of yourself, it becomes difficult to assess the pros and cons of any course of action. You're torn by self-doubt, and that is not an attitude you want to have when you're pushing the edge of the envelope.

Test pilots know that they live on the edge. One little flaw in an aircraft and it's curtains for them. But, they have full confidence in their ability to handle most of the things a cantankerous machine can throw at them. Things go wrong sometimes; things can always go wrong, that' life; but, believe me, these people live life to the fullest. They know how to grab the brass ring.

8. Traits of Successful and Fulfilled People (AKA Risk Takers)

Successful people, people who get the most out of life, have a number of character traits in common. If you've studied leadership, you will note that these are also the traits common to effective leaders. And that, my friend, is what most successful people are – leaders. Not necessarily leaders in the traditional sense of occupying formal leadership positions, but they are people who have nearly full control of their own destiny, and to who others look when the chips are down are something needs to get done.

Honesty - It really doesn't matter if you're leading from an official position, or just living your life, honesty is a trait that is absolutely essential if you're to be successful and live a life that is fulfilled. People must be able to trust your word if they are to follow you, or, in personal relationships, have any faith in you and what you say. Growing up in the 1940s and 1950s in a small rural town in East Texas, I noticed that the local farmers seldom worked with written contracts or agreements. Their philosophy was, "if I can't trust what you say, what difference will a signature on a piece of paper make." In those days, your word was your bond, and you were only as good as your word. Be honest to others, and to yourself, and you're on the way to living a life of fulfillment.

Integrity – Integrity is related to honesty, but involves much more. Honesty is in the things you say and do to others, mainly, but integrity is in you. It is in how you live your life, the things you do and say. It's not enough to just tell the truth; you must live the truth. Honesty is your reputation; how others know you, and what they say about you to your face. Integrity is who you are; it's about how you comport yourself when no one else is looking; it is the real you. A good example I like to use in my talks to young people about leadership is what people do when driving. It's honest on a crowded city street to obey all the traffic regulations – not to mention wise, but, what do you do when you're driving late at night with no other cars around, and you come to an intersection with a stop sign? No one's around to see you break the rules, and it looks clear. Do you blow through, or do you stop and make *sure* the way is clear before going on? That's what integrity is all about.

Self-confidence – Effective leaders; in fact, successful people in general; have loads of confidence in themselves. Sometimes, it seems to be arrogance or pride, and in some people that might be true. But, the successful, fulfilled person is quietly self-confident. She knows her limits, but is willing to test them to achieve her goals. I'm not referring to what often passes for self-confidence; the person who is willing to tell all and sundry about his outstanding talents; I'm talking about the person who simply 'makes a heap of all his winnings, and risks it all on one game of pitch and toss; who loses and begins again at his beginnings, and never breathes a word about his loss.' These words from Rudyard Kipling's poem, "If," have been with me (and I hope the poet's spirit will forgive me for paraphrasing him) since I had to memorize it for a school assembly when I was in elementary school many years ago.

Knowledge – Taking risks takes knowledge. Effective leadership takes knowledge. Learning should be a lifelong pursuit if you want to be successful. In fact, the constant pursuit of knowledge is a key trait of successful people. If you want to grab the brass ring, you have to know where it is, how far you have to reach to have a chance to snag it, and what some of the barriers are to that successful grab.

Courage – It goes without saying that venturing into new territory takes courage. Going where no one's gone before takes the ability to face your fears and doubts, and go on despite them. This is not just the courage that is normally associated with soldiers in battle, police officers in the line of fire, or firemen in a real fire; this is the courage to make unpopular decisions, to break from the pack and follow a different road; the courage to tell others what they might not want to hear, but need to hear.

Good communication skills – No matter how good your ideas might be, if you're unable to convey them to someone else so that they're understood, their worthless. Effective people are excellent communicators, orally, in writing, and in body language. Everything about them transmits a clear, easy to understand message: here's where I want to go, here's what I want to do. Good communicators are also good listeners and good observers. They're always aware of how others are receiving their message, and make adjustments as necessary to get that message across. A good example of poor communication happened to me in 1964, when I reported for officer training at Officer Candidate School in Fort Sill, Oklahoma. Having been on my first trans-Atlantic flight, followed by a two-day bus ride from Brooklyn to Oklahoma, I was tired and befuddled, and all the yelling and pushups we new candidates had to do that first evening didn't help matters. After a session of 'indoctrination' by those students who were senior to us, we were released to our barracks to prepare for our first inspection the following morning. A smarmy sounding upper classman joined us to give us his expectations of us; the lowest form of life. He carried a swagger stick, a little baton that was once favored by British military officers that is now outlawed in the US military, which he constantly tapped on the nearest handy surface to emphasize his points. I had the bad luck to have the bunk nearest the door, so I and my meager possessions provided the surface upon which he tapped. As he was explained to us how he wanted us to paint a perfect red circle on each of our boots, on the instep. As he spoke, he tapped my instep with each word. Now, I knew that this boob didn't know what he was talking about; he actually meant the bottom of the boot just in front of the heel. But, he kept tapping my instep, and I knew that he was tapping the correct part of my foot, just not the part he actually meant. Well, as luck would have it, later that night, I borrowed a bottle of red nail polish and complied with his instructions. The problem was, I complied with what he 'said' and what my mind was focused on rather than what he 'meant.' The next day, I proudly displayed two pairs of mirror-shined combat boots with almost perfect circles on - you guessed it - the insteps. I think I must have done over a hundred pushups that morning before breakfast, and that upper classman didn't appreciate my explanation that I'd done precisely what he said. His response was, "You puke; you know what I *meant*." Effective communicators don't make that assumption.

Dedication and Energy – Getting things done properly takes energy and persistence; getting things done that haven't been done before, or that are particularly challenging, will tax every mental, physical, and emotional resource you have. Effective people, though, don't let the difficulty of a task deter them. Somehow, they always seem to have that extra supply of energy down there somewhere they're able to tap when the going gets tough. And, they don't recognize the word 'impossible.' Again, from Rudyard Kipling's poem, "If,":

> If you can force your heart and nerve and sinew
>   To serve your turn long after they are gone,
>   And so hold on when there is nothing in you
>   Except the Will which says to them; 'Hold on!'

That is the mark of a person who succeeds against all odds.

Empathy – Risk takers aren't always the most sympathetic of people. But, one thing they do have; and this is true generally of successful people; is the ability to empathize with others. They might not agree with, or even like, what you do, or in most cases, don't do; but, they often understand better than you the reasons for it. The ability to see another's point of view, even when you disagree with it; probably more importantly, when you *don't* agree with it is critical to personal success. When you're taking an unpopular stance, it helps to know why it is unpopular. Taking risks, particularly in a work environment, can be mitigated to a degree if you can explain why you're doing so. But, if you're to convince the skeptics, that explanation has to be in terms of what they think and believe; not what you think and believe.

Vision – Effective leaders; successful people in general; have the ability to see what others not only can't see, but often can't even imagine. Being able to visualize a desired outcome is the first step in achieving it. Of course, as previously noted in communication skills; it helps if you can convey that vision to others.

Creativity – Risk taking is all about being creative. When one way doesn't work, or is closed, you take another. Successful people are inventive; they always seem to be thinking and acting outside the box; or, as one woman once said to me in describing her young son's 'out of the box' thinking; "He doesn't just think outside the box, he ignores the box entirely."

A Sense of humor – If you take risks, you will have your share of failure. Failure, though, is just a prelude to eventual success. Learning to laugh at your mistakes, while at the same time, you're learning from them, will help keep you trying. Laughter has a way of easing tension and putting things in perspective. If you can laugh at yourself, you will be a happier and more fulfilled person, whether you take risks or not. What's more, other people will enjoy being around you, and you're likely to find them laughing *with* you more often than they laugh *at* you. It's true what they say; laughter is the best medicine for almost every ailment.

The ability and willingness to take risks – Okay, I know you're probably thinking; this is a no-brainer; after all, this book is about taking risks. But, the ability and the willingness to venture into uncharted territory is a key character trait of most successful people. In fact, I'd even go so far to say, *all* successful people. Most children are born with it; just ask any mother; but, somewhere along the way, the system leeches it out of most people, leaving the 'play it safe,' 'follow the rules' mentality that infects most of our bureaucracies. Thankfully, the system fails with a few, and they grow up into the type that become test pilots, they introduce personal computers to the world, they invent the light bulb, or as Ben Franklin did, discover that lightning is actually electricity – they hang onto that quality we're all born with, and see each new day with wide open eyes, seeing possibilities that others miss, and taking advantage of them. They live life to the fullest, with no regrets or time to cry over failure; they're too busy looking for that next adventure.

Remember, you can never reach the stars unless you first reach *for* the stars. So, throw off those shackles of doubt and fear, and soar!

As you go through life, if you take chances, you'll fall down a lot; but, what matters is how many times you get back up and keep moving.

9. A Few Parting Words

You only have one life to live; and, it's your choice whether it will be a safe, play by the rules existence, never tasting the fruit of victory after challenging the impossible, the kind of reliable, humdrum existence that it the lot of far too many people on this earth. Or, knowing that you have only one chance at this life, you can saddle up, ride on the outside of the carousel and grab for that brass ring at every pass.

The choice is yours.

When I stood on that roadside over fifty years ago, waiting for the bus, I had no real idea what lay ahead. I had a vision of seeing the world, meeting new people and learning new things, but, beyond that, the future was a dense fog. The farther I traveled, though, and the more new things I experienced, the lighter and more transparent that fog became.

You can choose to follow the trail laid by others; that way is known and safe. You can even choose to travel the less-traveled path; there's a little risk there, but if someone else has already been that way, the risks are few in most cases. Or, you can choose to make your own trail; go where no one else has gone. That way lies great risks, but also great rewards.

You can believe the saying, "There, there be sea monsters and you'll sail off the edge of the world," and stick close to known shores. Or, like the Vikings who set out in long boats across the treacherous North Atlantic, or Christopher Columbus, who got lost trying to find a route to India, you can point your bow in a completely new and unknown direction. Just think what the world would be like if they hadn't dared.

In a few places in this book, I've quoted from Rudyard Kipling's poem, "If." This is one of my favorite poems, actually, it's my all time favorite piece of verse; so, I'm reproducing it here for you. Kipling was a product of his times, so the language might sound sexist, and it's difficult to be politically correct and write a good poem, as anyone who has written poetry will know, but what he says applies equally to men as well as women. I haven't mentioned specific women in this work, but such notables as Marie Curie and Amelia Earhart come immediately to mind – oh yes, and Joan of Arc. So, ignore the male references if you prefer, but pay close attention to the meaning.

IF

**If you can keep your head when all about you
Are losing theirs and blaming it on you,
If you can trust yourself when all men doubt you,
But make allowance for their doubting too;**

Grab the Brass Ring

If you can wait and not be tired by waiting,
Or being lied about, don't deal in lies,
Or being hated, don't give way to hating,
And yet don't look too good, nor talk too wise;

If you can dream – and not make dreams your master;
If you can think – and not make thoughts your aim;
If you can meet with Triumph and Disaster
And treat these two imposters just the same;
If you can bear to hear the truth you've spoken
Twisted by knaves to make a trap for fools,
Or watch the things you gave your life to, broken,
And stoop and build 'em up with worn-out tools;

If you can make one heap of all your winnings
And risk it on one turn of pitch-and-toss,
And lose, and start again at your beginnings
And never breathe a word about your loss;
If you can force your heart and nerve and sinew
To serve your turn long after they are gone,
And so hold on when there is nothing in you
Except the Will which says to them; 'Hold on!'

If you can talk with crowds and keep your virtue,
Or walk with Kings – nor lose the common touch,
If neither foes nor loving friends can hurt you,
If all men count with you, but none too much;
If you can fill the unforgiving minute
With sixty seconds' worth of distance run,
Yours is the Earth and everything that's in it,
And – which is more – you'll be a Man, my son!

Reading List

The following is a list of book that I've found particularly useful in my personal and professional life. They're not about risk taking, as such, but a careful reading will reveal that the willingness to 'go beyond the lines' is a key factor in being a successful and fulfilled person. Just as I hope that you will find some gem of information in this book, I feel certain that these books will have that one piece of information you've been needing to get out of the rut and onto a new path of adventure and achievement.

Kenneth Blanchard and Spencer Johnson, *The One-Minute Manager,* William Morrow and Company, New York, 1982. Although a book on management, the sections on delegation relate directly to risk taking. It takes confidence to allow subordinates to do things.

Donald T. Phillips, *Lincoln on Leadership,* Warner Books, New York, 1992. The discussion of how Abraham Lincoln approached leadership during the crucial periods of the Civil War are instructive for anyone who wants to know more about 'going boldly where no one's gone before.'

Warren Bennis, *Managing People is like Herding Cats,* Executive Excellence Publishing, Provo, UT, 1999. If you have time to read only a small portion of this short book, make it chapter 12, 'Ten Traits of Dynamic Leaders.'

Pete Blaber, *The Mission, The Men, and Me,* Berkley Caliber, New York, 2008. Written by a former Delta Force Commander who fought in Iraq, this book is all about taking risks.

Ann Miller Morin, *Her Excellency: An Oral History of American Women Ambassadors,* Twayne Publishers, New York, 1995. For women to excel in a profession that was formerly male-dominated takes guts, and lots of them.

Charles Ray, *Things I Learned from My Grandmother About Leadership and Life,* PublishAmerica, Baltimore, 2008. A short book on the principles of leadership that I learned from the woman who raised me; risk taking is implicit in every chapter.

_____, *Taking Charge: Effective Leadership for the Twenty-first Century,* PublishAmerica, Baltimore, 2009. The follow-on to *Things I Learned from My Grandmother.*

Charles Ray

About the Author

Charles Ray has been involved in leading and living life to the fullest since childhood. From being the youngest student to ever be elected student body president of his school, to experimenting with chemicals in a shed behind his house, he has blazed his own trail his entire life.

He served 20 years in the U.S. Army, with two tours in Vietnam during the war, and assignments in Germany, Korea, and several locations in the United States. While most people think of the military as a hierarchical organization which gives the individual little room for maneuver, he managed throughout his career to defy conventional wisdom, enlisting with only a high school diploma from a segregated school system, he retired at the rank of major, with experience in unconventional warfare, psychological operations, civil affairs, public affairs, and instruction.

After retiring from the army, he joined the U.S. Foreign Service, with postings to China, Thailand, Sierra Leone, Vietnam, Cambodia, and Zimbabwe, serving as U.S. Ambassador to Cambodia and Zimbabwe, and was selected as the first U.S. Consul General in Ho Chi Minh City, Vietnam in 1998, establishing the first official American presence in that city since the fall of Saigon in 1973. He also served as Deputy Assistant Secretary of Defense for Prisoners of War/Missing Personnel Affairs, overseeing the US Government effort to account for those missing from our past wars, and having responsibility for policy relating to rescuing those who fall into captivity. His capacity for taking risks continued. He again defied conventional wisdom by taking assignments that, though fascinating, were thought not to be career enhancing. His record of assignments and commendations attest to the invalidity of that conventional wisdom.

A prolific writer, he has authored two other books on leadership as well as several works of fiction and a book of photography of southern Africa. He is a frequent contributor to media, print and electronic and has been included in several poetry anthologies.

A native of Texas, he now calls Maryland home, and lives just outside Washington, DC with his wife, Myung.

www.ingramcontent.com/pod-product-compliance
Lightning Source LLC
Chambersburg PA
CBHW061517180526
45171CB00001B/220